d Like to
ake Your Goods

Rick,
I came to Campsing
one summer shortly
after you had been
there... I spent the next
month known as
"Rick-not-Redt."
I had a good time
nonetheless.

1/19/06
@ F.A.S.
Northridge.

the
poet's experience
on his honeymoon in
Paris, Rome and Venice

by Rick Lupert

I'd Like to Bake Your Goods

Ain't Got No Press

Design, and Layout ~ Rick Lupert
Front Cover ~ "The Wedding" by Marc Chagall
Photographs ~ Rick Lupert
Author Photo ~ Addie Lupert

Thanks to Bernie and Sara, Gregory and Mary, David and Elizabeth, Steven and Debbie, Uncle Robert, Mom, Brendan, Elizabeth, Barry, Danny, Craig, Patti, Amélie, Amit, Carlye and David and all those who launched us into bliss.

(818) 904-1021

or

15522 Stagg Street
Van Nuys, CA 91406

or

Rick@PoetrySuperHighway.com

or

http://PoetrySuperHighway.com/

First Edition ~ First Printing ~ January, 2006

Printed by InstantPublisher.com
United States of America

ISBN: 0-9727555-5-1 $10.00

For Addie, the source of all poetry.

"When love is not madness, it is not love."

Pedro Calderon de la Barca

"Lunch kills half of Paris, supper the other half."

Charles De Montesquieu

"Every city has a sex and an age which have nothing to do with demography. Rome is feminine. So is Odessa. London is a teenager, an urchin, and, in this, hasn't changed since the time of Dickens. Paris, I believe, is a man in his twenties in love with an older woman."

John Berger

"Rome was a poem pressed into service as a city."

Anatole Broyard

"I had rather be first in a village than second at Rome."

Julius Caeser

"Venice is like eating an entire box of chocolate liqueurs in one go."

Truman Capote

"Though there are some disagreeable things in Venice there is nothing so disagreeable as the visitors."

Henry James

"Love. Exciting and New. Come aboard. We're expecting you."

Paul Williams

Paris

June 30th, June 30th

for Richard Brautigan

It is June 30th 2004,
or as the French would say

The thirtieth of June, two thousand and four
but in French

The Eiffel Tower and the moon
make a nice pair

I'm rediscovering carbohydrates
like Sherman Oaks is going out of style

On French TV, a cereal box with eyes
lives in a pineapple house under the sea

We live above a giant train station
with tunnels that could take us clear to seventeen-eighty-nine

We take a trip on a night boat on the river
I sleep through most of it

but am awake for dessert an hour later
Profiteroles and Berthillion Ice cream

I am concerned there are two many L's
in the name of that ice cream

Today we will meet the Mona Lisa
I doubt she will remember me

The Shower is So Small

in our hotel room,
by the time we're finished with the soap
we're already at the Louvre

Today

we will visit many dead people
I'm wearing closed toe shoes

Yeast

We launch into July
like a baguette sticking
out of a Parisian's underwear

Architecture

The buildings here are old
unlike in Los Angeles where
we still have to burp them

Lizard King

Our tiny hotel room
with the paisley wallpaper
and the red carpet and
the window overlooking Avenue Victoria
and the paisley wallpaper
and the bathroom made for one
and the blood red carpet
with our big bed and smooth ceilings
surrounded by paisley wallpaper
and a TV remote control
and electricity and air
and one big bed for two
with a window to Paris
unless you're outside
in which case it's a third floor portal
to our paisley wallpapered world

Football

Last night someone won a soccer game we guess
as the car horns and cheering and flag waving Parisians
float into our one-am hotel window
and coax us to sleep

Paris

It stays light until after ten pm
which we're not used to
but, I guess, has something to do
with how the planet works
and science and the sun or geometry,
or maybe God just wants people
to see this city clearly
for a couple more hours

Unintentional Not Haiku

Soon we will eat
we eat every day here
it's like a disease

Football

This time it's a blue and white flagged team that's won
we can tell because they carry the flag through the
alleyways of the Latin Quarter, trapping us with
their French hooting and hollering

Addie

insists we kiss
everywhere in Paris
She really doesn't need
to insist

Addie

almost waves her wedding ring into the Seine
as a boatful of people pass under us, I assure her
there's no more romantic place for us to lose our rings

Language Barrier

I'm pretty good at French
but still manage to confuse
the word for "bottle" as I order
a boat-full of water

It is the Second of July

and we are in our clean Paris hotel room
a block south of Rue de Rivoli

It rained today and we put on our hats
like speed hat wearers

My feet hurt like the French Revolution
My legs are sore like a stone spiral stair way

to the top of Notre Dame. My head is confused
like too much chocolate fondu

We had to cut up our own fruit
while the chocolate was on the way

we are looking forward to
a variety of crepes

I wonder if she is still in the museum
after all these years

All painted and naked
We are avoiding Italian food until Italy

where we figure
they'll specialize in it

The Eiffel Tower is big my love
but not as big as my love for you

Luggage Siblings

It's so cute that we have matching suitcases
I wonder if they're married and that's where
our smaller luggage came from.

P.S. Our backpack was adopted

After Viewing the 'Before Impressionism' Section at the D'Orsay

one can infer that, back then,
everyone spent a lot of time naked

Paris is infested with Americans

We are all ashamed
not speaking to each other

as we overhear our English
conversations in museums

or relieved when we're
seated next to each other in Fondu restaurants

or curious to where are
all the French people anyway

Cheese Now

Paris is at its best when you're sitting
in front of a plate of cheeses

and you've left your diet on the West Coast
of a completely different country

We are in a cafe called Les Deux Musees (The Two Museums)
named so as it sits in front of two museums

We only went in one of the museums
where upon encountering an image of ducks

Addie grabbed me and said
"ooh duckies! Quack Quack!"

Addie was three years old once
and hasn't looked forward since

She comments at the next painting "Now there's a baguette"
referring to the sword the man is holding

The world would be a better place
if we beat our swords into baguettes

and ate them on the Left bank of the Seine
I eat cheese with my wife

Chopin in an Old Church

The pianist performs humble as a river
We are in one of Paris' oldest churches
built when the memory of Jesus was young
like America

You can hear every noise,
the scuffling of a foot
the scratching of my pen
the dueling concertos
from the piano
and someone's cell phone

The acoustics of a stone cathedral
make you feel like you're there

The pianist's fingers
are as confident as rain

Friday night with the Jews in East Paris

We are interviewed like we're getting on a plane to Israel
Inside, the people are wearing the familiar artifacts
The walls are decorated with the familiar language
The Chazan performs the familiar prayers

On the way out we thank the guard for letting us in
with an inappropriate joke about not being terrorists
He doesn't smile and I am reminded that
security personnel find nothing funny

Discovered

At breakfast I caught you licking your coffee cup
"I'm making sure it doesn't drip" you giggle
Soon we are both licking our coffee cups
eyeing each other suspiciously

In the Monet Museum (Marmotan)

You might die
looking for a paper towel in Paris
I thought as a waterlily wept

Walking from the Musee Marmotan Monét

Can we stop at a bakery?
I'd like a baked good.

I'd like to bake your goods
like I did last night. Remember?

Yes. It was hot.
Hot like it would need to be
to bake goods.

Where the Hell Are We?

An hour outside of Paris
we got off the train
survey the French countryside
Praise God for the opportunity
to have seen this spot
and get back on another train
back to town

So what if Claude Monet's house in Giverny
is only accessible by
a completely different train

New Diet

for Steve Martin

I'm only eating cheese and bread in Paris
and occasionally something green
It might be spinach,
but they call it something different here

The French have a different word for everything

Fourth of July in Paris

We visit the little Statue of Liberty
It turns out to be bigger than we thought
Addie had wanted to shake her hand
but instead only manages to
look up her skirt

All the Weight

I lost before the wedding
I'm finding again in Paris
It's like parts of me
started the honeymoon
months ago

Rome

Right Away, Confusion

Instead of towels in the hotel
there are giant wash cloths
I'm not sure whether to shower
or bake a lasagna

History

In the Piazza Navona
I am listening the sound of four rivers

drown out a man screaming
in Italian like he was at Vietnam

The waiters laugh at him like
they moved to Canada to avoid the draft

We miss seeing a Raphael
because the Christians are at it again

Most of Rome on the floor
except for buildings with crosses

haiku

From the train to town
a small fire on a hill
The empire still burns

Inner Trunk

Addie makes like an elephant
under a statue of an elephant
it's what Bernini had in mind

At the Arch of Constantine

for Brendan Constantine

I thought of you
while standing under Constantine's Arch

The ancient Roman's saw you coming
two thousand years in advance

"Some day a man will come" they thought
"whose words will charm even the Vestal Virgins"

It's no wonder the Forum is surrounded by Greek columns
The Christians tried to pull them down with rope and faith

When they failed, they simply put crosses on top
and called it a day

I wonder if I tied a rope to your head
would I end up with a new synagogue

I stand under your Arch
surrounded by white noise

and you with the weight of the Empire
wrapped around your head like leaves

Burden

The guide tells us that Jewish slaves
brought back by Titus built the Colosseum

It's no surprise

What ancient structures
didn't my ancestors build?

Tired

Addie has had enough of ancient Rome
and as far as she's concerned

all the Empire's problems could be erased
by one scoop of Gelato

It's seven thirty pm
The Pantheon stands erect.

In the Pantheon

There are signs which state
"Is forbidden to sit on the floor"
Most of these signs

are surrounded by visitors
sitting on the floor
kind of like the Italians

lighting up
wherever they see
a "no smoking" sign

Hot in Rome

I would kill for a shower
at the Spanish Steps
Well, not so much kill as
be very appreciative of
Still, I read in the tour book
That someone was killed
on these steps. Maybe
the person who killed him
was really hot.

Pace

There are multi-colored flags
hanging from windows all over Rome
but the one I liked best
was the one hanging from the building
across the street from the Vatican
as if the owner was saying
"Hi Pope. I'm Gay, and I'm your neighbor
Have a nice day. I'll see you at the block party."

In the Vatican Men's Bathrooms

There are no toilet seat covers
or toilet seats
This is also the case with the women's bathrooms
(I checked with my wife)
The Roman Catholic Church
frowns on number two

On our way to the Underground Dead

Addie says
"I don't think I have the right shoes for the Catacombs"

It's a niche market:
shoes made for walking under ground

Not Wanting to Overdo it on Pasta

and because we miss Paris,
we stop in to an English Tea house
at the bottom of the Spanish Steps
for iced tea and cheese.
We'll experience all of Europe
with this one meal.

Chiesa dei Santi Vincenzo e Anastasio

We are drawn to this place
across from the Trevi Fountain

because the book says its crypt contains
the hearts and lungs of former Popes

We've already eaten
so we figure it's safe

The church is surrounded by
pizzerias, glass shops and

The United Colors of Beneton
We catch the end of mass inside

and then humbly approach the alter
and ask if we can see the crypt

He says it never opens
He has been here a year

and hasn't seen the inside
and anyway, he hears

There is nothing to see
We seem sweet to him

so he asks us where we're from
"Los Angeles" we say

and he responds with "aaah"
and then nothing

like everyone else in Europe
speechless because maybe

we're movie stars
sweet movie stars

when all we really want
is to see the guts of dead Pontifs

The Eternal City

They eat gelato
with their backs towards the Pantheon

Gesticulate on cell phones
oblivious to Neptune and dead Popes

Ride their scooters without a glance
towards the fountains and arches

No-one appreciates
the treasures of their own city

The Romans are like their statues
without eyes

Inkblot Test

Addie sees a street sign
and isn't sure if the image on it
is a flower
or a bird smoking a cigar

At the Shelley and Keats Memorial

I'm sorry Shelley,
we missed memorializing you in person
by fifteen minutes.

We stand at the bottom of the Spanish Steps
at your death house in front of a closed door
and an electric button that says
Museum

Et Tu Addie?

Relaxing on our bed before dinner
My wife wants me to go shower
so she can have one of my pillows

untitled

for Anthony P. Hann

Circle of life
The week Tony Died
Jane's Addiction brokeup
and I got married
Circle of Life

Covenant

Thousands of Greek and Roman marbles
an albino who's who of the ancient world
You can tell right away
that none of them were Jewish

Not Horns

Most people see them as horns coming out of Moses' head.
That's why when you meet someone who's never met a Jew
They look curiously at your head, and ask to see them.
Now that I've seen the original in Rome, I can tell them
Michelangelo was somewhat awkward
when carving rays of light

The Acoustics in the Pantheon

When I sneeze in there
it bounces off the walls
hundreds of people are silent
and looking at me
for a brief moment
The empire is mine

Si

After three nights of struggling
with your non-existent Italian

When you've said something correctly in Italian at a restaurant
the waiter will say "si" like you've given him the right answer
to a trivia question.

So what if he brings you the wrong kind of melon
You've had a triumphant moment of "yes"

The Tiber River is Open All Night

like a 7-11
You can buy anything on its banks
Like a fern at three AM
in a Sherman Oaks pharmacy

Tear Down the Walls

We proudly tour the Vatican
walk into any cathedral unnoticed
boldly ask to see the crypts of some
But when Addie walks into the only Synagogue in town
with a Kipah on her head
She gets dirty looks from the locals
The end of the Jewish People
will not come from the outside.

Rare finds in Rome

Empty Piazzas
Non-smoking sections
Quiet

Haiku

Italian is a
language like a circus, but
with less elephants

Humid

Water
source of life
veins of the city
a pretty good idea
until it's rubbing off the air
onto your body

Oh Rome

three nights were not enough
to satisfy you (with your)

Trastevere, and your Borghese
and your museum of crime and punishment

all for the next time
Every city deserves at least a week

we leave with a few photos
and a stomach full of you.

Venice

Would it Help if I Got Out and Pushed?

Since the city is surrounded by it
You'd think there wouldn't be
a problem with water pressure
in the hotel

Something Addie Said

Give me that pen.

Behold, the Future

Our first floor hotel room has a balcony
which overlooks the intersection of two small canals
which will make it easier for me to present
my midnight naked serenade
to passing gondoliers

Doing Laundry in Venice

means airing out my shirts
on the balcony

I'm proud of this display of shirts
Addie suggests I'll be even prouder

when a wind comes and I see my shirts
floating down the Grand Canal

At This Point in the Trip

Addie isn't just asking for my pen;
She's threatening to take it.

Do Yourself a Favor

when in Venice at dinner time
www.bistrotdevenise.com

Choose Your Own Metaphor Poem

We are served the finest meal we've ever had
by a man who:

a)   knows more about food than you do
     about your grandchildren

b)   has a more intimate relationship with food
     then we do with our lungs

c)   offers more personal service
     then a colon doctor

d)   _____

     _____

     _____

In Piazza San Marco

Dueling classical outfits
cause the tourists to run back and forth

across the square to their different renditions of
New York, New York

We take seats based solely on proximity
Pay the Ten Euro Music fee

Addie has mint tea and I order
water with bubbles, my Italian favorite

We spend money in Europe
like we're making a movie

We have the best seats in the house and our quartet
is rounded out by a piano and an accordion

Listening to classical music in Europe
is like growing a baby from a human being tree

The violinist's bow is frayed
They're taking a break now

My water gets less bubbly
with each passing empire

Music

The clarinetist uses the same reed
for both of his clarinets, Addie notices
I suggest one gets used to
putting one's mouth on just one thing
and we leave it at that

And For So Many Other Reasons

You are the kind of person
who knows the difference
between reeds and bows
and who'll tell me so
I don't publish a book of poems
which refers to the wrong parts
of the wrong instruments
providing more fuel to my naysayers
I love you for that

Concert at the Guggenheim

It's not that the music is bad
the instrumentalists are hitting

all the right notes
But why *those* notes?

A leaf falls in front of the guitarist
one can only assume this concert

is making the trees die
months early

I'm positive the bassist is playing
too many notes. Whiskers on kittens.

The guitarist moves his mouth silently
while he plays . . . like reverse karaoke

The keyboardist . . . well I hate to be cynical
but this elevator is going nowhere

This is so new-agy it feels retro
Did I mention the keyboardist

is dressed like a karate master?
Things like that don't matter

I feel like a leaf falling
months before my time.

The Mating Call of the Gondolier

Because gondolas don't have horns or brakes
when they approach a blind intersection, they cry out "Oi-yee"
to alert potential other gondoliers around the corner
and avoid slicing one of their gondolas in half
along with their precious tourist cargo.

I suggest a similar system for humans on sidewalks
or any walkway. A series of guttural cries
to avoid mishaps caused by oblivious walkers
who have no idea who they are or where they are going.

This would work well in museums too
as people creep backwards in front of priceless art
for a better view, unaware of the Chinese family
they are about to topple. Imagine in the Louvre,

or perhaps the streets of New York City,
a new soundtrack of gratuitous noises,
echoing into the sky, forever replacing
"Hey I'm walkin' here."

I Ask Addie to Remember the Phrase

"The mating call of the gondoliers"
so she can tell it to me in the morning
and I'll remember to write the last poem.

At the first morning bells of the tower in St. Mark's Square
She rolls over to me and says "The mating of the gondoliers!"
which is a completely different vision.

Naomi

Wedding becomes as long as birthday
we encounter old St. Louis friend in,
of course, Jewish Ghetto

We're dining on her card tonight
with gift wine and gift bruschetta
and gift meloncello

Discover drinking and drinks
like a newborn chocolate fiend
in Switzerland

Return to restaurant of first night
which we've romanticized
beyond all possible expectation

The three of us re-encounter
food guru, or food-ru
as we like to say

More peach drinky drink
and three desserts which would make
the Doge leave the palace alone

It is good to meet old friends
and to be
a new friend

We learn the food man's name
Giovani. He offers to wrap our sweets
in bacon

He jokes because
he is the food guru
with the yang sense of humor

we all look forward
to next encounter in California, or Venice
or the next Jewish Ghetto

Last Words

I am eaten by insects in Venice
left with only enough energy and flesh
to scribble this down

Sorry Bruno

We have made a non-friend of the hotelier
having refused his tour twice now

Perhaps it is him who turned off our hot water
or sent the insects to our bed

to eat away the last bits
of our changing American flesh

Modern Antiquity

The canal water at night
is still like a statue
of canal water

The Bubbly Floors in Every Venice Building

That's what happens when
you build your civilization
on mud

Thank You Haiku

We will toast to you
tonight Naomi, as we
fall to Venice sleep

Some Thoughts On Modes Of Travel And The Travel Industry While On A Boat From St. Mark's Square

for Derrick Brown

1

Boat drivers stand
which makes it a different experience
from car drivers
who sit

2

When an airline purchases an airplane
from a manufacturer of airplanes
is the plane delivered or is it picked up?
In either case, who pays for the airfare
to either travel to pick up the plane,
or travel back home after delivering it?

3

Gondolas are black
and all the gondoliers have big muscles
because they spend a lot of time
gondoliering

4

I know a man who lived on a boat once
and at a different time was also a gondolier.
Some day, I think he'll move to space.

About the Wagon

I stumble through the alleys
and over bridges

with my wife in one hand
and a bottle of wine in the other

Now this is a picture
I would love to see

Dear Los Angeles

I'm writing to you from Venice
Not your hippie laden Venice,
child of the Santa Monica Bay,
But Venice, Italy, where from my
hotel first floor window, I can see
the intersection of two canals
one of which floats south
under the Bridge of Sighs
where once thieves and
enemies of the empire
would take their last glimpse
of the blue Venice Lagoon
before heavy iron and stone
became their eternal city

I too have a last glimpse now
at this often stagnant water
shared equally by motorized boats
and historic ones powered only by
the girth of striped shirted men

Los Angeles, the stars are quiet here
unlike yours which make a sound
the world can hear, even if
you can't see them at all

My wife is finishing up and soon
we'll be on our way to you
to risk another six months on your ground
before the next big televised disaster
Every city has its risks. Did you know Venice
has been sinking for almost a millennium?

We're getting out while we can
Try to stay in one piece
Every time we mention you to anywhere else
Their eyes glimmer with the picture of you
covered with the Pacific

It is almost time to go.
We'd like to pre-order one of your famous
Apple Pies. Your large plates with
a mountain of potatoes.
I have to close my suitcase now.

Los Angeles

Los Angeles

I scrape the last whiskers of Venice off my face
watch them swivel into underground Sherman Oaks

Where they go from there,
I do not know

Maybe the ocean
or a place where such things are investigated.

The mosquito bites are fading
along with the memories of canals and cathedrals

I rinse the blade
The honeymoon is over

about the author

Rick Lupert has been involved in the Los Angeles poetry community since 1990. He served for two years as a co-director of the Valley Contemporary Poets, a twenty-three year old non-profit organization which produces a regular reading series and publications out of the San Fernando Valley. His poetry has appeared in numerous magazines and literary journals, including *The Los Angeles Times, Chiron Review, Zuzu's Petals, Caffeine Magazine, Blue Satellite* and others. He is the author of nine other books: *Paris: It's The Cheese, I Am My Own Orange County, Mowing Fargo, I'm a Jew. Are You?, Stolen Mummies* (Ain't Got No Press), *Lizard King of the Laundromat, Brendan Constantine is My Kind of Town* (Inevitable Press), *Feeding Holy Cats* and *Up Liberty's Skirt* (Cassowary Press). He serves on the Artist and Community Advisory Council of Beyond Baroque Literary Arts Center in Venice, California. (Though he's not sure how that happened or what it means.) He has hosted the long running Cobalt Café reading series in Canoga Park since 1994 and is regularly featured at venues throughout Southern California.

Rick created and maintains the Poetry Super Highway, a major internet resource for poets. (http://PoetrySuperHighway.com/)

Currently Rick works as a music teacher at Temple Ahavat Shalom in Northridge, CA and as a freelance graphic and web designer.

Rick's Other Books

STOLEN MUMMIES
Ain't Got No Press
February, 2003

BRENDAN CONSTANTINE IS
MY KIND OF TOWN
Inevitable Press
September, 2001

up liberty's skirt
Cassowary Press
March, 2001

FEEDING HOLY CATS
Cassowary Press
May, 2000

I'm a Jew, Are You?
Cassowary Press
May, 2000

MOWING FARGO
Sacred Beverage Press
December, 1998

Lizard King of the Laundromat
The Inevitable Press
February, 1998

I Am My Own Orange County
Ain't Got No Press
May, 1997

Paris: It's The Cheese
Ain't Got No Press
May, 1996

For more information: http://PoetrySuperHighway.com/